The "Stand Up Paddle & Yoga" Sutras

Reinventing The Art Of Yoga

By Vie Binga & Tim Ganley

Dedication

This is for our Parents, Viola & Jean, Mary & Apostolos.

- Tim& Vie

Preface

The first time I (Vie) fell off of a paddleboard, I was practicing sun salutations. I knew right then and there thatthis was going to be a lifelong passion. The time was summer of 2006, and the place, Fort Desoto on the Gulf Coast of Florida. We had just finished taking a group out for KaYoga (a term coined by Tim…) to Shell Key, a tiny island nearby.

We were using our 2 newly purchased paddleboards (Jimmy Lewis) that we had ordered from North Carolina. At that time, no one in our area was carrying paddleboards. The popular belief at the local surf shops was that paddleboarding was just another fad. Time has proven they were mistaken.

We had seen the curiosity on people's faces when they saw us standing while paddling, as opposed to sitting. I looked at Tim and said, "I bet I can do more Sun Salutations than you." Tim decided to take me up on this challenge and he fell in at the 9th Sun Salutation while I kept going, until I "willingly" fell in at number 20.

Years later, we came to realize that at that moment, every one around us had witnessed the sea-grass roots of what came to be SUP & Yoga (Stand Up Paddle & Yoga.)

People were having so much fun trying out our 2 Jimmy Lewis paddleboards that within a few months we ended up switching our kayak fleet into a SUP fleet consisting mostly of the now extinct Imagine Surf Eco Hybrid Surfers (Hybrid as in SUP/Kayak.)

It was amazing to watch the enjoyment on people's faces as they were standing and gliding across the water making eye contact with the dolphins and manatees who were playing all around them. Little did we know that the amazement we were witnessing then was minimal compared to what we felt when we watched them practice yoga on their paddleboards.

I cannot think of a more rewarding feeling than having played a positive part in another person's life-changing experience. Having introduced thousands of people to Stand Up Paddle & Yoga and having certified hundreds of SUP & Yoga Teachers, there are no words to describe the human bond that Stand Up Paddle & Yoga helps create.

And here we are, attempting to document our personal experience, so we can introduce as many people as possible to the magical portal of Stand Up Paddle & Yoga.

A word of advice - For Every One

Water activities are an assumed risk sport. You assume all liabilities for your participation in anything described in this book. This book does not take the place of appropriate instruction in yoga, paddling, swimming and life saving techniques. It is the ultimate responsibility of the paddler to judge their ability and act accordingly. This is what we found, over the years, to work best for us in keeping our clients and friends safe while teaching SUP & Yoga on flat-water. You may have to add or subtract accordingly depending on your area and waterway.

A word of advice - For SUP & Yoga Teachers

You cannot successfully teach anything you do not understand or believe in.

So, we highly recommend to continuously practice, practice, practice *proper* technique, your selves. Contrary to popular belief, practice does *not* make perfect. Practice makes permanent. Please, practice wisely…

An ongoing process…

This book will continue to improve and grow as the Stand Up Paddling & Yoga sport evolves. In the meantime, we would love to hear back from you on what worked and what did not. If you have a better way of performing one of the tasks or you have found a piece of gear that makes your life easy, please, let us know!

We wish you a positive life-changing journey!

Thank you for reading!

- Vie & Tim

January, 2016

INTRODUCTION

The Water is calling you... Are you going to answer?

Water, water, water... One of the main four elements that has been worshiped in every single civilization and culture for thousands of years.

Depending on our location, job, family and social obligations, our modern day lifestyle might have taken us away from water more often than not.

But somehow, no matter how challenging it may be for us, we seem to always find a way to get close to a moving body of water, whether that is a waterfall, a lake, a river, a creek, the beach, the ocean... We plan holidays, vacations, weekend getaways, walks, runs, bike rides, centered around the magical presence of water.

Science says that we are at least 70% water, a fact that seems to explain, our natural attraction to this magnificent source of life.

Japanese scientist Masaru Emoto in his revolutionary work "The Hidden Messages in Water" says that "water teaches us in a very clear way how we must live our lives. The story of water reaches from every individual cell to encompass the entire cosmos."

So Get Up and Stand Up!

Wouldn't it be great if instead of being "close" to the water, you were able to seamlessly stand on the water absorbing as much as possible of the scenery and the life unraveling all around you?

It seems that our ancestors, out of necessity, and mainly for survival had figured out numerous ways to make that happen. Evidence dates back to at least 9,000 years ago.

Now Let Your Board Be Your Mat

According to Juan Carlos Santana, founder of the Institute of Human Performance, in Boca Raton, Florida, as human beings, we are hard wired for the following four pillars of movement:

1. Standing & Locomotion
2. Level changes in the body's center of mass
3. Pushing & Pulling
4. Rotation

Proper stand up paddleboarding, innately, involves movements 1, 3 and 4. Incorporate yoga poses (asanas) to stand up paddling and you arrive to one of the most natural and complete types of movement ever experienced: Stand Up Paddle & Yoga (SUP & Yoga)

Beauty & Strength in Body, Mind & Soul

It is no coincidence that C4, the first dedicated paddleboard manufacturer, has had four core values as part of their mission:

- Balance
- Endurance
- Strength
- Tradition

This is what proper stand up paddleboarding assists in cultivating. This is also what the Patanjali Yoga Sutras teach. Both disciplines give us a variety of tools we can use to create beauty and strength in body, mind and soul.

Yoga on the stand up paddleboard adds yet another powerful and revolutionary instrument to our toolbox. This is what can and will, if we allow it, drastically accelerate our path of our never-ending quest for grace under pressure.

Since there are too many books and not enough time, we will keep this book short and the point. What follows in this book will give you the essential knowledge and tools needed to safely experience that which has already changed so many lives around the world…

How To Use This Book

This book is written based on the following premise:

<u>When on the water, you are a Stand Up Paddler first, a Yoga Practitioner second.</u>

This means that you are already a **competent** Stand Up Paddler / Guide or working on becoming one. Having said that, we highly recommend that you download our book, <u>**"Walk On Water - A Guide To Flat Water Stand Up Paddling" from Amazon.com**</u>.

Now that we are all on the same wavelength, pun intended   we can establish how to make the best use of this book.

This book starts with a few words on the magic, science, and practical considerations that you need to be aware of, before actually hitting the water.

It then moves on to a detailed description of several key poses. These poses have been carefully selected and modified to best fit the paddleboard. The cues have been outlined in enough detail and do not require any prior yoga or fitness experience. If you are already a seasoned yoga practitioner, we suggest, as a personal challenge, that you see how these cues can blend into your own personal practice.

This book would not be considered a complete introduction to SUP & Yoga without two very practical sections adapting Breath-Work and Meditation Practices for the water.

The section on SUP & Yoga boards and gear will teach you how choosing the proper equipment can improve the efficiency of your time on the water.

At the end of this book there are links to invaluable resources (videos/blogs/courses) that will expose you to many different aspects of SUP & Yoga.

Remember, the possibilities are endless!

The Ānanda Factor

"If you are not in the moment, you are in the water."

Ānanda in Sanskrit (the language that the original yoga texts were written in) means bliss. It is that state of inner surrender, where we have transcended reason and feel fully inspired.

In modern day terminology it is also referred to as the zone, or the flow.

A Scientific Perspective

Psychologist Mihaly Csikszentmihalyi (who coined the term "flow" in 1975) says that when in the flow, "every action, movement and thought follows inevitably from the previous one, like playing jazz."

Now, we do not have to learn to play jazz or even like jazz to appreciate this concept.

Csikszentmihalyi helps us understand the zone or flow using a structure of eight dimensions to describe the experience for individuals across occupations, demographic groups and cultures.

These dimensions are listed by Csikszentmihalyi (1990) as: (a) clear goals and feedback; (b) balance between challenges and skills; (c) action and awareness merged; (d) concentration on task; (e) sense of potential control; (f) loss of self-consciousness; (g) altered sense of time; and, (h) autotelic (self-rewarding) experience.

These dimensions are deemed to constitute the conditions necessary for the occurrence and continuation of the zone.

A Yogic Perspective

These eight states are also the conditions described as the foundation of the dhāraṇā, dhyāna and samādhi , the three final states of the eight limbs of yoga according to the Patanjali Sutras.

> "These three when practiced in regard to one object, constitute samyama. Through the attainment of samyama comes the light of knowledge… Samyama should be first applied to gross things, and when one begins to get knowledge of the gross, slowly, by stages, it should be applied to finer things. ... This is a note of warning not to attempt to go too fast." -*Raja Yoga by Swami Vivekananda, Ramakrishna-Vivekānanda Center New York (p. 184))*

A Surfer's Perspective

Following Swami Vivekānanda's warning of "not going too fast", we would like to simplify our view of the Ānanda Factor and understand it as reaching a meditative state while your body is fully engaged and your mind fully aware.

As Gerry Lopez (one of the great surfers/shapers and yogis of our time) stated

> "We became hippies and got into yoga and that whole self realization thing and started to realize that those moments when you were completely focused on riding a wave are actually kind of spiritual... religious moments."

Without further ado, let's get you started on your quest for the Ānanda Factor.

Risk & Reward

In today's day and age, with all the attention that has been brought into the physical aspect of yoga, we all understand that any yoga pose can hurt you and any yoga pose can help you, depending on your circumstances.

We will break down your circumstances into 3 major categories:

- Your idiosyncrasies (skeletal, muscular, proportions, etc.)
- Your physical condition at the time (injuries, illnesses, fatigue, etc.)
- The time and place of your practice (season, time of day, studio, park, beach, etc.)

So, when it comes to yoga, like every other great activity in life, sooner or later, it all becomes a matter of personal preference. What that means is that even though there are countless styles out there, you as a practitioner (whether novice or seasoned) know what is right for you and your own circumstances.

The Ocean Cannot Be Tamed

Bringing your practice on the water, adds two significant parameters to the "Time and Place" category above. The context now becomes very different. You are in an uncontrolled environment and on an unstable surface.

Uncontrolled Environment

What do we mean by "uncontrolled environment"? Think of your own home. Isn't it the most controlled place for a yoga practice? That's of course assuming that puppies, kitties, etc. are all welcomed on your mat. :-)

Now, let's go to a studio, with other practitioners close to you, and then out on the park or on the beach, with unexpected "visitors" and sounds. Now picture yourself on a paddleboard anchored in a pool, or on a lake or even out on the open water. We've had anywhere from curious and playful dolphins and manatees to unaware jet skiers and power boats say 'hi' to us during corpse pose. :-)

Whether the "distractions" are part of nature or not, situational awareness, while on the water, becomes even more important.

> "Situational awareness is the ability to always pay attention to what is going on around you, monitor your surroundings and recognize changes."

Unstable Surface

What do we mean by "unstable surface"? As you can tell, the term is self-explanatory. The real question should be "why is it even worth talking about?" Think of you standing. When you are standing, without even you applying any conscious effort, your body is involuntarily engaging muscles in order to keep your bones from collapsing. It is our natural and irreversible reflex response against gravity.

Now think of you standing on an unstable surface. You are going to involuntarily and voluntarily engage even more muscles to keep you from loosing your balance and falling over. In fact, this is the case whether standing, sitting, lying down, moving or not, on the unstable surface. This muscle contraction inherently helps you develop strength. So yoga on a paddleboard should be viewed as primarily targeting strength and balance, not flexibility.

The Ratio Of The Pose

Taking into consideration the three major categories above we can now approach every pose from a whole new perspective and develop a deeper understanding and appreciation for its essence. We look at what we call, the Ratio of the Pose, defined as follows:

The Ratio of the Pose = Risk / Reward

The *Risk* represents the probability of something going "wrong" and in case that happened, how "wrong" that might be, as in minor injury, permanently debilitating or even fatal. The Risk is not associated with the skill level of the practitioner. It is measured based on the inherent nature of the pose.

The *Reward* represents the benefits you actually receive from performing this pose.

Ideally, the Ratio of a pose should always be less that 1, in other words, the Reward should outweigh the Risk.

How Do You Determine The Ratio Of A Pose?

Learning to evaluate the Ratio of a pose is highly specialized and well beyond the scope of this book. However, the following four principles always apply.

- ◆ The Ratio of a pose is higher in an uncontrolled environment than in a controlled environment.

- ◆ The Ratio of a pose on a stable surface is lower than on an unstable surface.

- ◆ Due to our daily lifestyle and habits (sitting for long periods at time, typing, texting, etc.) poses that target strength have statistically been shown to have lower Ratios, i.e. smaller risk of injury and more benefits.

- ◆ Due to our lack of strength, poses that target flexibility have statistically been shown to have higher Ratios, i.e. bigger risk of injury and less benefits.

The Sweet Spot

Definition of the Sweet Spot

If you have already read our **"Walk On Water - A Guide To Flat Water Stand Up Paddling"** and feel comfortable with the concept of the Sweet Spot, feel free to glance over and/or skip this section. Otherwise, thoroughly understanding this section is going to make a world of difference for your SUP & Yoga practice.

The sweet spot is the area of your paddleboard where the following 3 are happening simultaneously:

- ◆ You feel very stable standing.
- ◆ Neither the nose nor the tail of your board is sinking in the water.
- ◆ The rails are even.

The location of this area is typically surrounding the center of mass of your board but its dimensions depend on the architecture and construction of your board. Typically, the handle of the paddleboard is within the Sweet Spot of the board.

As you are probably already suspecting, what makes a good yoga / fitness board is a very large sweet spot.

The quickest way to start becoming familiar with a board you have not used before is to identify its Sweet Spot.

How to find the Sweet Spot

Once you are standing comfortably on your board, walk a few inches forward until the nose of the board starts sinking.

Now, start walking back until the tail of the board starts sinking.

You have just established the space in between the nose and the tail, where neither the nose nor the tail is sinking. That is the length of the Sweet Spot of your board.

Standing within that area, keeping your feet at a comfortable distance (at least hip distance apart) start shifting them to either side of the board, i.e. towards the rails. Notice how far your can go without the rails becoming uneven.

You have just established the space in between the rails that defines the width of the Sweet Spot of your board.

Now What?

During your practice on the board, whether standing, kneeling, seated or lying down, keep in mind that staying within the sweet spot is going to make life easier. This however, does not mean that you should not step outside the sweet spot. What it means is that if a pose seems to be more challenging than on land, the first thing to check is that your center of gravity is within the sweet spot of your board.

Yoga poses are divided in 2 major categories:

- Symmetrical (or Bilateral)
- Asymmetrical (or Unilateral)

A symmetrical pose shares the load between two limbs, whereas an asymmetrical pose places effort on only one limb.

Examples of Symmetrical Poses: Plank; Goddess; Camel;

Examples of Asymmetrical Poses: Side plank; Warrior II; Wild Thing;

Both symmetrical and asymmetrical types of poses have great benefits and are necessary for a well-rounded practice.

Symmetrical poses are more forgiving on the paddleboard than asymmetrical. Asymmetrical poses really test your understanding of the sweet spot, your focus and core control.

Final Tips

Things to keep in mind while using this book…

- For asymmetrical poses, we give you the detailed cues on one side. Remember to do both sides. :-)

- The cues are such that you do not need to use your paddle at all for any of the poses. If you wish to use your paddle for extra stability during your standing poses, you are more than welcome to.

- For the poses that ask you to lie on your back, you have the option to lie down with your head either towards the nose or towards the tail of your board. We recommend that you choose the side that will get your hair wet the least. :-)

- You can always try your poses on land first, and then take them on your board. Either way, have fun, be creative, and don't be afraid to get wet!

The Staple Poses

"As in a river the masses of water are changing, before you every moment, and new masses are coming, taking similar form, so it with this body. Yet the body must be kept strong and healthy; it is the best instrument we have." - *Raja Yoga by Swami Vivekananda, Ramakrishna-Vivekananda Center New York (p.28)*

Staple Poses got their name due to their simplicity and their importance. We could spend hours and several pages analyzing the "simplicity" and "importance" aspects but that is a full subject of its own. For the moment being, think of the Staple Poses as your bread & butter and let's get ready to have some fun!

The poses below are not listed in any particular order. Start where you want, skip what you want, add what you want, change what you want, but most importantly get on the water today and do something!

All of these poses have Ratio's that are less than 1, i.e., the reward is higher than the risk. We also refer to them as "low-maintenance" poses.

Table-Top

Come into kneeling, within the Sweet Spot of your board.

Bring your knees underneath your hips and your hands underneath your shoulders, creating a flat back.

Spread the fingers apart, push through every single finger, push through both hands.

If you feel any pressure on your wrists, make fists, with the knuckles pushing on your board and the wrists straight. Do not bend your wrists.

It is a pose you can hold for as long as you like while breathing in and out through your nose.

Figure 1: Table-Top

Cat

Start in our Table-Top pose.

On an exhale, tuck your chin and round your back towards the sky, pulling your belly button away from your board as much as you can.

On an inhale, return to Table-Top or follow with the Cow pose.

Figure 2: Cat

Cow

Start in our Table-Top pose.

On an inhale, drop your belly towards your board and look up towards the sky, squeezing your shoulder blades together as much as you can.

On an exhale, return to Table-Top or follow with the Cat pose.

Figure 3: Cow

Plank Pose (High Push Up Pose)

Start in our Table-Top pose, facing the nose of your board.

Walk you hands further forward and your feet further back towards the tail so that your hands are underneath your shoulders and your knees behind your hips, creating a plank-like formation from your knees to the top of your head.

If you can, lift your knees off your board.

If your knees are off the board, your butt should be about 1" higher than the rest of your body to protect your lower back.

Your hands should be right underneath your shoulders.

If you feel any pressure on your wrists, make fists with the knuckles pushing on your mat and your wrists straight. Otherwise, spread your fingers as far apart as you can pushing into every single finger, pushing through both hands. This should relieve pressure off the shoulders.

Focus at the area below the belly button and starting there, use it to tighten your whole core as if your are pushing the board away from you. Remember that the butt is part of our core.

Lift the heels as high off the board as you can for more of a core challenge.

Keep your shoulders away from your ears.

Look about half a foot in front of you, breathing in and out through the nose.

For more of a challenge in terms of balance and strength, keep your feet closer together. For less of challenge, separate your feet further apart.

Hold for about 4 breaths.

To get out of the pose, push yourself back into our Downward Facing Dog or our Wide Legged Child's pose.

Figure 4: Plank with knees on the board

Figure 5: Plank with knees off the board

Downward Facing Dog (Down-Dog)

Start in our Plank pose (High Push Up pose), facing the nose of your board.

Without shifting your hands and feet, raise your hips as high up towards the sky as you can, creating an inverted V formation with your body and fully extending your spine.

Make sure there is no pressure on your neck, so keep your gaze where it feels good for your neck.

Your heels do not have to touch the board.

Work towards extending your legs as long as there is no pressure on your lower back.

Focus on engaging the outside of your thighs, as if the rails of your board are pulling them away from each other.

Keep pressing your hands onto your board just like in our Plank pose.

Spread your shoulder blades apart and using your upper body, pretend your are pushing the board away from you.

Bring your attention to the area below your belly button and starting from there, engage your whole core.

Hold for about 4 breaths.

To get out of the pose, come back into our Table-Top and transition into a Cat-Cow flow.

Figure 6: Downward Facing Dog

One Legged Downward Facing Dog (One Legged Down-Dog)

Left Side

In down-dog, on an inhale, keeping your arms straight and your hips even, lift your left foot off the board and extend your left leg up and back towards the sky.

Your left foot can be pointed or flexed.

Keeping your hips as even as possible, squeeze your glutes and inner thighs. The more even your hips, the more stable you stay on the board.

Push your hands into your board, as if you are pushing the board away from you. Keep spreading the shoulder blades apart, extending your spine as much as possible.

Relax your neck looking towards wherever it feels good for your neck and keeps you stable.

Keep your full core engaged and focus in particular at the area below the belly button. Keep it as lifted as possible.

Hold for approximately 4 breaths focusing on nose breathing.

On an exhale, lower your left foot on the board going back into our down-dog.

Prepare for the other side.

Figure 7: One-legged Downward Facing Dog – Left Leg Raised

Wide-Legged Child's Pose

From our Table-Top, on an exhale, bring your toes together and your heels apart, separating your knees as much as possible.

Lower your butt towards your heels and as close to your deck pad as possible.

Reach forward with your arms, towards the nose of your board.

Hold for about 4 breaths while breathing in and out through your nose.

To get out of the pose, inhale back transitioning into our Table-Top or Downward Facing Dog.

There are two Wide-Legged Child's Pose Variations you may also enjoy:

- ◆ Make fists with your hands and rest your forehead on your stacked fists.
- ◆ Rest your forehead on your stacked forearms.

Figure 8: Wide-Legged Child's Pose

Bird Dog – Left Leg and Right Arm extended

Come into our Table-Top facing the nose of the board.

On an inhale, extend your left leg back towards the tail of your board.

Keep your left foot flexed (not pointing), in order to use more glutes.

Keeping your core tight (glutes included) and without allowing the hips to shift on either side, extend your right arm forward so the palm faces the board.

Hold for 4 breaths. Remember that the deeper you breathe, the more balanced you stay.

To get out of the pose, on an exhale, lower the left knee and right hand on the board, transitioning in our Table-Top.

Prepare for the opposite side (right leg & left arm.)

Figure 9: Bird Dog with left arm and right leg extended

Chaturanga Pose (Low Push Up Pose)

Start in our Plank pose with your knees on or off the board.

Tighten your whole core (yes, that includes your butt), bend your arms, and keeping your elbows by your sides, lower your upper body as close to the board as you can, only allowing your chest and chin to touch the board (if needed), not your abdominal area or your hips.

Your goal is for your whole body, to be as straight as a staff, hovering about 1/2 – 1″ off the board without any pressure on your lower back.

Keep your hands right underneath your shoulders.

Keep your elbows as close to your sides as possible.

Keep your toes tucked under.

Your knees can be on or off your board.

If your knees are on the board, then your whole body, from your knees to the top of your head should be as straight as a staff, and hovering about 1/2 – 1″ off the board without any pressure on your lower back.

If this is still too challenging for you, you can allow your chest and chin to touch the board for support. Your hips should still stay off the board, hovering about 1/2 – 1″ off the board.

Hold this pose for 4 breaths, focusing on nose breathing.

To get out of the pose, using your knees for support if needed, push yourself up into our Plank pose and transition into our Downward Facing Dog or Wide Legged Child's pose.

Figure 10: Chaturanga with knees, chest and chin on the board

Figure 11: Chaturanga with knees on the board, chest and chin off the board

Figure 12: Chaturanga with knees, chest and chin off the board

Cobra

Come into our Chaturanga (Low Push Up Pose), with your knees on or off the board, facing the nose of your paddleboard.

Keeping your elbows by your sides, squeeze your glutes as much as you can, brace the rest of your core and raise your upper body towards the sky.

Keep your knees and thighs and feet on the board.

Now loosen up your glutes to take pressure off your lower back.

Your toes can be tucked under or have the top of the feet on the board. Depends on how your deck pad feels against your feet.

Your arms can be bent or straight, depending on how much of an arch feels good on your lower back. The straighter the arms, the more intense the back bend.

Keep your elbows close to your body.

Keep your hands flat on the mat underneath your shoulders, spreading the fingers apart.

Using your hands and your upper body strength, push the board away from you.

Keep your shoulders down and back, away from your ears.

To avoid unnecessary pressure on your neck, look up with your eyes, not with your neck.

Hold for no longer than 4 breaths, focusing on nose breathing.

To get out of the pose, using your knees for support transition into our Wide Legged Child's Pose or Downward Facing Dog.

Figure 13: Cobra with toes tucked under

Upward Facing Dog (Up-dog)

Come into our Chaturanga (Low Push Up Pose), with your knees on or off the board, facing the nose of your paddleboard.

Keeping your elbows by your sides, squeeze your glutes as much as you can, brace the rest of your core and raise your upper body towards the sky.

Raise your knees, thighs and hips off the board.

Now loosen up your glutes to take pressure off your lower back.

Your toes can be tucked under or have the top of the feet on the board. Depends on how your deck pad feels against your feet.

Keep your arms extended and hands flat on the mat underneath your shoulders, spreading the fingers apart.

Using your hands and your upper body strength, push the board away from you.

Keep your shoulders down and back, away from your ears.

To avoid unnecessary pressure on your neck, look up with your eyes, not with your neck.

Hold for no longer than 4 breaths, focusing on nose breathing.

To get out of the pose, set your knees on your board and transition into our Wide Legged Child's Pose or Downward Facing Dog.

Figure 14: Upward Facing Dog

Superman

From our Table-Top, lie down on your belly with your legs together and your arms behind you along side of your body.

On an inhale, engage your whole body, especially your glutes, chest and back and raise your whole body (except your belly button) as high off the board as possible.

Use your glutes to help you lift your legs. Keep extending the legs towards the tail of your board and keep raising them.

The more you engage the glutes, the less pressure on your lower back.

Use your chest and back to help you lift your upper body and your arms. Open up your chest towards the sky, keeping the shoulders down away from the ears.

Using your belly button, push the board away from you.

To avoid extra pressure on your neck, look up with your eyes, not your neck.

Hold for approximately 4 breaths focusing on nose breathing.

On an exhale, lower your whole body towards the board and immediately using your hands for support, bringing your toes together, your heels apart and separating your knees as much as possible, going into our wide legged child's pose.

There are some Superman Variations you may also enjoy. You can modify by adjusting:

- ◆ The width of the legs, you can keep them anywhere, from touching to as far apart as you like.
- ◆ The position of the arms, you can keep them extending forward towards the nose of your board, to the side towards the rails or behind you and even interlaced reaching towards the tail.

Figure 15: Superman

Dolphin

Come into our Downward Facing Dog, facing the nose of the board.

Without shifting the feet, lower your forearms onto your board, bringing your elbows underneath your shoulders. Interlace your fingers.

On an exhale, tighten your core even more and raise your hips as high as possible towards the sky.

On an inhale, lower your hips, shifting your shoulders forward.

To get the most benefits out of this pose, your butt should stay above the rest of your body for the whole movement.

Do not let your weight collapse on your shoulders and your arms. Use your core. Focus at the area below the belly button and use it to engage the rest of your core.

The skin of your forearms and elbows should not feel irritated after this pose. :-)

Repeat this flow for 4 – 8 breaths.

To get out of the pose, on an exhale, transition into our Downward Facing Dog by straightening the arms, or Wide-Legged Child's pose if needed.

Figure 16: On an exhale, raise your hips towards the sky

Figure 17: On an inhale, lower your hips and shift your shoulders forward

Bridge Pose

Lie on your back so that your glutes and lower back are within the Sweet Spot of your board.

If you do not want your hair to get wet, you can lie down with your head towards the nose of your paddleboard. :-)

Bend your knees and set the feet on your board, at hip distance apart, so that your knees are in line with your heels. Keep the feet completely parallel, toes forward.

Bring your arms along side of your body, palms facing the board.

Squeeze your glutes, and on an inhale, lift your hips as high up as possible towards the sky.

Our Bridge pose is all about the glutes, not the hamstrings. If at any point, you feel the hamstrings taking over, drop the butt onto your board, squeeze it and raise it up again.

The more you push your heels and the outside of the feet onto the board, the more you engage the glutes.

The more you engage the glutes, the less pressure on your lower back.

Keep your knees from rolling in or out. They should stay inline with your heels.

Hold for 4 breaths.

To get out of the pose, with control, lower your butt onto your board and hug your knees into your chest, gently rocking from side to side, without falling into the water. :-)

Figure 18: Bridge

Sea Scallop

Lie on your back with your glutes and lower back within the Sweet Spot of your board.

If you do not want your hair to get wet, you can lie down with your head towards the nose of your paddleboard. :-)

Keeping the knees slightly bent to take pressure off your lower back, raise the legs towards the sky, keeping the feet flexed.

Keeping the belly as tight as possible, raise your head, shoulders and arms as high off your board as you can, trying to reach your legs with your arms.

You can keep your head up or let it drop back, whichever way feels best on your neck.

Do not grab your legs with your hands, that would create leverage and it would be cheating. :-)

Keep reaching your legs towards your head and your upper body and arms towards the legs, closing your body as a sea scallop would close its shell.

Hold for approximately 4 breaths focusing on nose breathing.

To get out of the pose, bend your knees and lower your upper body onto the board. Hug your knees and rock side to side.

Figure 19: Sea Scallop

Reverse Table-Top

Come sitting within the Sweet Spot of your board facing the nose.

Bring your hands on the board, behind your hips.

The fingers can face the tail, the nose or the rails depending on which way feels best on your shoulders, chest and back. You can even make fists if you need to, with the knuckles on the board and the wrists straight.

Bend the knees and set the feet on the board, parallel to each other and at hip distance apart.

Squeeze the butt as much as you can and on inhale lift the hips as high as possible.

The knees should be straight above the heels and the feet should be pushing the board away from you in order to lift your upper body as high as possible.

Our reverse table-top is all about the glutes, not the hamstrings.

The knees are not moving but they are squeezing towards each other as if you are holding a heavy weight in between them.

You can drop the head back or keep it up, which ever way feels best on your neck.

Keep breathing in and out through the nose, lifting the hips and opening up the chest towards the sky.

Hold for approximately 4 breaths.

On an exhale, gently, with control, lower the butt on your board, adjust the pelvis to tilt forward and follow with our seated forward fold.

Figure 20: Reverse Table Top

Boat Pose

Come sitting within the Sweet Spot of your board, facing the nose.

Place your hands on your deck-pad, just behind your hips.

Bend your knees and on an inhale, engaging your core for support, lift your feet off your board.

It is perfectly okay to round your lower back, but not your upper back.

Keep your shoulders down, away from your ears.

For more of a challenge, you can lift your hands off your deck-pad, you can support your thighs with your arms, or your can keep your arms reaching forward.

Make sure there is no pressure on your lower back.

Our Boat pose targets mainly the belly area of your core. So, to feel it there, adjust how much your legs are raised and your knees bent.

To make it more intense extend the legs and raise them, to make it less intense, bend the knees and lower the feet.

Keep the chest out and your gaze up towards the horizon.

Hold for 4 breaths, breathing in and out through the nose.

To get out of the pose, on an exhale, lower the feet onto your board, and hug your knees into your chest straightening your back, before transitioning into our Reverse Table Top.

Figure 21: Boat

Side Plank - Right Side

Start in our Plank Pose (High Push Up Pose) facing the nose of your board with your knees on or off your deck pad.

Check that your belly is within the Sweet Spot of your board.

Bring your right hand underneath your forehead, extend your other arm up towards the sky, and using your core as much as possible, lift and turn your hips so your whole body is now facing the left rail of your board.

Make sure that your right hand, knee and foot are inline within the Sweet Spot of your board.

Your right knee can be on or off your board. If you are going to keep your knee on the board, it needs to stay behind your hip, not underneath your hip. That would be cheating and in the long run it may also hurt your hip.

Your feet can be stacked (less support, more challenging) or you can have one in front of the other (for more support).

If your right wrist is bothering you, see if you can make a fist with the knuckles against the board and your wrist straight. Otherwise, keep spreading the fingers apart pushing on the deck pad through every single finger and through the whole hand. That should take pressure off your shoulder.

Keep your neck relaxed gazing towards wherever it feels best on your neck and helps you stay balanced.

Squeeze your glutes, and engage your obliques, and the rest of your core as if you are trying to lift your whole body of the board. Do not let the hips sink.

Keep your whole body centered and strong. If you loose focus, you could fall in the water. :-)

Hold for about 4 breaths, targeting nose breathing.

To get out of the pose, bring your left hand on the board, going into our Plank Pose.

Get ready for the other side.

Figure 22: Side Plank with right hand and right knee on the board

Figure 23: Side Plank with right hand on the board and right knee off the board, feet stacked together

Starfish Pose – Right Side

Come into our Table-Top pose, with your upper body within the Sweet Spot of the board, facing the nose.

Adjust the position of your right hand on the board. Some people prefer the hand underneath the forehead and others find it easier out to the side. It is different for every one. As long as you do not get outside the width of the Sweet Spot. :-)

If the wrist is bothering you, you can make a fist with the knuckles on the board and wrist straight. Otherwise, keep spreading the fingers apart, pushing through every single finger and the whole hand.

Place your right knee underneath your right hip.

You can keep the top of your right foot on the board or tuck your toes under, whichever way helps you stay stable.

On an inhale, engaging your whole core, raise your left knee off the board, and your left hand off the board.

Extend your left leg back towards the tail and your left arm up towards the sky, opening up your whole body to face the left rail or your board.

Keep your raised foot flexed (not pointing) in order to target more glutes.

Do not let your raised leg fall forward or lower, keep it aligned with the rest of your body.

Keep your neck comfortable looking up towards the sky or straight into the horizon.

Do not let your weight fall onto your joints, fully engage your core.

Hold for about 4 breaths.

To get out of the pose, on an exhale lower your left knee and left hand onto your board, transitioning into our Table-Top pose.

Prepare for the other side.

Figure 24: Starfish with right hand and right knee on the board

Mountain Pose

Come standing within the sweet spot of your board.

Bring the feet at hip or shoulder distance apart or further if needed, for more balance.

Keep your feet pointing forward and parallel to each other. Do not let the toes turn out and the heels in.

Keep your knees soft, and your thigh muscles lifted and turned out.

Squeeze your glutes.

Draw the stomach in tight.

Keep your shoulders down and back, squeeze your shoulder blades together.

Your palms can face the nose of the board, the tail, or your thighs, which ever way feels best on your shoulders.

Keep your chin parallel to the board, lift the gaze slightly up into the horizon.

Breathe in and out through your nose and smile.

Keep pushing the bottom of both of your feet solid on the board, as if you are pushing the board away from you.

Experiment with pushing through the outside of the feet, lifting the inner arches and squeezing your gluten as much as you can and the back of your legs.

Hold for about 4 breaths.

Lift your toes, spread them apart and set them back down. Perform this twice.

Figure 25: Mountain Pose

Exalted Mountain Pose

Start in your Mountain pose, within the Sweet Spot of your board.

On an inhale, raise your arms up over your head.

Keep your arms strong, and your shoulders down and back, away from your ears.

Keep your elbows from bending.

Hold for about 4 breaths, gazing towards the horizon or the sky depending on what feels best for your neck.

To get out of the pose, on an exhale, bring your hands to the heart center, palms touching and back into your Mountain Pose.

Figure 26: Exalted Mountain

Standing Crescent Moon - Right Side

Start in our Exalted Mountain Pose, within the Sweet Spot, facing the nose of your board.

Interlace the fingers and bring your hands into the steeple pose.

Drop your shoulder blades (away from your ears) and work towards keeping the elbows straight.

On en exhale, lift the spine, and push your hips towards the left rail of your board, taking your arms towards the other direction (right rail of your board), creating a crescent moon shape.

Work at keeping your chest straight and your back from arching.

Do not let your arms fall forward.

Hold this pose for about 4 breaths, keeping your chin slightly up.

To get out of the pose, inhale back to center, into Exalted Mountain, keeping your arms up and as straight as you can.

Repeat on the opposite side.

Figure 27: Standing Crescent Moon - Left Side

Standing Crescent Moon Variation - Right Side

Start in our Standing Crescent Moon, facing the nose of your board, with your hips towards the left rail and your arms reaching towards the right rail.

Separate your hands and grab your left wrist with your right hand.

Take your hips further to the left rail and your upper body along with your arms further to the right.

Pull on your whole left arm, not just the wrist, keeping the arms as straight as you can.

Keep your shoulders down, away from your ears.

Feel the extension of your whole left side of your body.

Keep your upper body from twisting, or collapsing forward and your arms from falling forward.

Keep your neck fully relaxed and your chin slightly up, gazing towards the horizon.

Hold for about 4 breaths breathing in and out through your nose.

To get out of the pose, separate your arms and inhale back into Exalted Mountain.

Prepare for the other side.

Figure 28: Standing Crescent Moon Variation - Left Side

Standing Back-Bend

Start in our Exalted Mountain pose, within the Sweet Spot of your board, facing the nose.

If you feel any low back tension, place your hands behind your lower back to support it.

Otherwise, keep your arms up over your head and interlace your fingers into the steeple pose.

Keeping your glutes loose, gently, push your hips and thighs forward feeling your back-bend, without forcing it. We are targeting joint mobility, so for your low back to get the most benefits out of this pose, it is important that you do not squeeze the butt.

You can drop your head back or keep it up, which ever way feels best on your neck.

Keep breathing in and out through your nose.

If you need to open the mouth to breathe, while in your back-bend, please, do so.

Hold for no more than 4 breaths.

To get out of the pose, gently, inhale back into our Exalted Mountain. On an exhale, either bring the hands to the heart center, palms touching releasing into your Mountain pose or follow with our Standing Forward Fold, which ever way feels best on your lower back.

Figure 29: Standing Backbend Variation, with hands separated as opposed to interlaced

Standing Forward Fold

Start in our Exalted Mountain Pose within the Sweet Spot of your board, facing the nose.

On an exhale, with your stomach tight and your knees bent as much as needed, push your hips and thighs back folding your upper body towards your lower body. Keeping the knees bent takes pressure off your lower back.

Your hands do not have to touch the deck pad.

Bend your arms and grab elbow to elbow, creating a box with your arms.

Let your head, shoulders and shoulder blades just hang in there.

Keep your chin as close to your chest as you can, and use gravity to help you fully extend your spine.

Hold for no more than 4 breaths, using every exhale to go even deeper into the pose.

To get out of the pose, release your arms, interlace your fingers into the steeple figure, and keeping your knees bent (to take pressure off your lower back) and your stomach tight, inhale all the way up into our Exalted Mountain.

Figure 30: Standing Forward Fold

Standing Forward Fold Variations

Bring your arms behind your legs and use your arms and legs as leverage to pull your upper body towards your lower body.

Keep bicycling your feet lifting one heel at a time off your deck pad.

If you wish to go even deeper into your pose, push your big toes onto the board and rotate your thighs inward.

Figure 31: Standing Forward Fold Variation

Chair

We consider this pose (squat) the lowest common denominator of human movement. In order for us to stand, pick things up, and even sit on the toilette we must first be able to squat. Most of us, as Westerners, have lived a very sedentary lifestyle. With school, work, TV, computer games, etc. our bodies have adapted to sitting. When this happens, our hips and legs become tight and our glutes weak. Lower body strength is essential.

The squats are one of the easiest ways to help counter act the chair. They are fundamental to any strength program and they are the first line of defense against weak hips and knees. The squats or chair pose can be performed in numerous ways. in order to challenge the body and create muscle confusion. To limit your practice to one or two types of chairs is not only limiting your body's full potential but in may also increase the risk of injury.

In this section we are going to explore the foundational paddleboard squat:

Come standing into our Mountain Pose.

Push through the outside of the feet, lifting the inner arches and squeezing your gluten as much as you can and the back of your legs.

Keeping your knees soft, on an inhale breath raise your arms up towards the sky and on an exhale keeping your hips as far back as you can, sit as low as you can while your upper body is still straight (chest not rounding) and your heels solid on the board.

Your knees can go past your toes.

If you feel too much pressure on your low back keeping your arms extended up, bring them parallel to the board or hands at heart center.

Keep looking straight ahead into the horizon, chin slightly up. Hold the pose for about 4 breaths focusing on nose breathing.

To get out of the pose, inhale all the way up into exalted mountain and exhale into mountain.

Figure 32: Chair

Low Lunge – Left Foot Forward

Start in our Table Top with your upper body within the Sweet Spot of your board.

On an inhale, bring your left leg forward, softly setting your left foot on your board in between your hands. You should not hear your foot land on your board.

If your foot does not make it all the way forward, no worries!! Use your left hand to grab it and bring it forward. Keep doing this and some day your foot will just show up there on its own!

Keep your back knee (right) on the board and as far back towards the tail of your board as you can. So, it should not be directly under your hip.

Your back foot can be pointed (top of the foot on your board) or flexed (toes tucked under), whichever way feels best for you.

Keep your hands on your board.

Keep your neck happy looking towards the horizon.

Check the nose and the tail of your board and make sure neither one is sinking.

You are now in your Low Lunge pose.

Hold for approximately 4 breaths focusing on nose breathing.

Gently bring your left leg back going into our Down-dog.

Prepare for the other side.

Figure 33: Low Lunge with Right Foot Forward

High Lunge – Left Foot Forward

Start in our Table Top with your upper body within the Sweet Spot of your board.

On an inhale, bring your left leg forward, softly setting your left foot on your board in between your hands. You should not hear your foot land on your board.

If your foot does not make it all the way forward, no worries!! Use your left hand to grab it and bring it forward. Keep doing this and some day your foot will just show up there on its own!

Keep your back knee (right) off the board and as far back towards the tail of your board as you can. So, it should not be directly under your hip.

Your back foot should be flexed (toes tucked under).

Keep your hands on your board.

Keep your neck happy, looking towards the horizon.

Check the nose and the tail of your board and make sure neither one is sinking.

You are now in your High Lunge pose.

Hold for approximately 4 breaths focusing on nose breathing.

Gently bring your left leg back going into our Down-dog.

Prepare for the other side.

Figure 34: High Lunge with Right Foot Forward

Lizard – Left Leg Forward

Start in our Low Lunge, with your left leg forward. Tuck your back toes under, so your back foot is flexed.

Take your left foot out to the side towards the left rail of your board and turn it out at about 45 degrees. Keep your left knee as much in line with your left foot as you can.

Keep your back (right) knee behind your right hip, not underneath.

Place both hands inside your left foot, and pretend you are using them to push the board away from you so that your hips shift as far back towards the tail as possible.

Separate your hands wider than shoulder width and bend your elbows, turning the elbows out, towards the rails of the board.

Lift your shoulders and chest and keep them parallel to your board.

Engage your lower belly, hips, glutes and thighs so that your pelvis stays as even and low to the board as possible, without touching your board.

Your back (right) leg and your right hip may tend to drop, do not let them. Your front (left) leg and hip may tend to lift, do not let them. That may throw you off your board and into the water!

Keep extending your hips and thighs while fully engaging your chest, back, glutes and the rest of your core as if you are trying to use all of your strength to push your board away from you.

Hold for approximately 4 breaths focusing on nose breathing.

To get out of the pose, bring your left arm on the outside of your left leg, and use it to slowly move your left foot in between your hands coming into your Low Lunge pose. Once there, transition into our Table Top and prepare for the other side.

- As a Lizard Variation and for more of a challenge, get your back knee off the board.

Figure 35: Lizard with Right Leg Forward

Figure 36: Lizard Variation with back knee off the board

Figure 37: Lizard Variation, different angle

Extended Lizard – Left Leg Forward

Start in our Lizard – Left Leg Forward Pose.

Your back foot is flexed, so toes are still tucked under.

Straighten the right elbow and place your right hand onto your board, in line with your right shoulder.

If your right wrist is bothering you, see if you can make a fist with the knuckles against the board and your wrist straight. Otherwise, spread the fingers apart pushing on the deck pad through every single finger and through the whole hand. That should take pressure off your shoulder.

Raise your left arm over your head, and fully extend it towards the sky.

Fully engage your upper back.

Keep your chest, belly and hips facing the left rail of your board and even the sky if possible.

Keep your shoulders away from your ears and your neck relaxed looking up towards wherever helps you stay stable on your board.

Keep your right knee on the board for less of a challenge, or raise it off the board for more of a challenge.

Do not allow your right foot to turn, keep the heel facing the tail of the board.

Engage your thighs, hips, glutes and the rest of your core so your weight is not collapsing on your joints.

Hold for approximately 4 breaths focusing on nose breathing.

To get out of the pose, bring your left arm on the outside of your left leg, and use it to slowly move your left foot in between your hands coming into your Low Lunge pose. Once there, transition into our Table Top or Downward Facing Dog and prepare for the other side.

Figure 38: Extended Lizard, Right Leg Forward

Twisted Lizard – Left Leg Forward

Start in our Lizard – Left Leg Forward Pose.

Lower your right forearm onto the board, if you can. If not, straighten the right elbow and place your right hand onto your board, in line with your right shoulder.

If your right wrist is bothering you, see if you can make a fist with the knuckles against the board and your wrist straight. Otherwise, spread the fingers apart pushing on the deck pad through every single finger and through the whole hand. That should take pressure off your shoulder.

Fully engage your upper back.

Keep your right knee on the board. Squeeze your glutes and engage your thighs so your weight is not collapsing on your knee.

Bend your right knee, flex your foot and reach back with your left hand, palm facing away from you.

If you can reach the foot, grab the outside of your right foot with your thumb on the instep and fingers wrapping around the top. Otherwise, bring your left hand behind your low back, with the palm facing away from your body.

Keeping the hips even, twisting from your obliques, open up your revolved torso towards the left rail of your board and the sky.

If you are holding your foot, kick your foot into your hand.

Keep engaging your core, so you are not letting your weight collapse on your joints.

You can let your head drop back or keep it up, whichever way feels best on your neck and helps you stay stable on your board.

Hold for approximately 4 breaths focusing on nose breathing.

To get out of the pose, bring your left arm on the outside of your left leg, and use it to slowly move your left foot in between your hands coming into your Low Lunge pose. Once there, transition into our Table Top or Downward Facing Dog and prepare for the other side.

Figure 39: Twisted Lizard, Right Leg Forward

Low Crescent Warrior – Left Leg Forward

Start in our Low Lunge Pose with your right leg back, facing the nose of your board and your upper body within the Sweet Spot.

Raise your upper body and your arms towards the sky, keeping your shoulders away from the ears.

Your front knee is straight above the heel and your front thigh parallel to the mat.

Your back knee should be behind your hip, not underneath, for more of a challenge.

To get the most benefits out of this pose, keep your hips as low as possible. Keeping your hips low and your lunge deep, is also assisting you to stay more balanced on your board.

Activate your butt, taking the bulk of the effort off of your legs. Push your front heel onto the board feeling the left side of the butt. Push the back thigh towards the tail of your board feeling the right side of the butt.

Your arms are strong as if you are holding the weight of the heavens.

If that is too much pressure on your lower back, bring the hands to the heart center.

Your back foot can have the toes tucked under or the top of the foot on the board, depends on how the deck pad feels on your foot.

Keep your chin and your gaze slightly up.

Hold the pose for about 4 breaths focusing on nose breathing.

To get out of the pose, bring your hands on your board transitioning into our Low Lunge and Downward Facing Dog.

Prepare for the other side.

Figure 40: Low Crescent, Right Leg Forward

High Crescent Warrior – Left Leg Forward

Start in our High Lunge Pose with your right leg back, facing the nose of your board and your upper body within the Sweet Spot.

Raise your upper body and your arms towards the sky, keeping your shoulders away from the ears.

Your front knee is straight above the heel and your front thigh parallel to the board.

To get the most benefits out of this pose, keep your hips as low as possible. Keeping your hips low and your lunge deep, is also assisting you to stay more balanced on your board.

Activate your butt, taking the bulk of the effort off of your legs. Push your front heel onto your board feeling the left side of the butt. Planting your back toes onto your board, push the back heel towards the tail of your board feeling the right side of the butt.

Your arms are strong as if you are holding the weight of the heavens.

If that is too much pressure on your lower back, bring the hands to the heart center.

Keep your back leg as straight as you can.

To get the most out of this pose, and to protect your hips in the long run, do not allow your back heel to turn in either direction, keep it straight.

Keep your chin and your gaze slightly up.

Hold the pose for about 4 breaths focusing on nose breathing.

To get out of the pose, bring your hands on your board transitioning into our High Lunge and Downward Facing Dog.

Prepare for the other side.

Figure 41: High Crescent, Right Leg Forward

Crazy Crescent Warrior – Left Leg Forward

Start in our High or Low Crescent Pose with your right leg back, facing the nose of your board and your upper body within the Sweet Spot.

Use your right arm to keep your hips and your upper body straight by wrapping it across your waist through the front of your body, reaching to your left oblique muscles.

With your left arm, keeping your left shoulder down, make 4 large circles clockwise and then 4 large circles counter-clockwise. Target full range of motion.

Now use your left arm to keep your hips and your upper body straight by wrapping it across your waist through the front of your body, reaching to your right oblique muscles.

With your right arm, keeping your right shoulder down, make 4 large circles clockwise and then 4 large circles counter-clockwise. Go for full range of motion.

Come back in our High or Low Crescent Pose.

To get out of the pose, bring your hands on your board transitioning into our High or Low Lunge and then Downward Facing Dog.

Prepare for the other side.

Figure 42: Crazy Crescent, with Right Leg Forward Using Right Arm

Figure 43: Crazy Crescent with Right Leg Forward Using Left Arm

Flying Crescent Warrior – Left Leg Forward

Start in our High (or Low Crescent) Pose with your right leg back, facing the nose of your board and your upper body within the Sweet Spot. If you are starting in the Low Crescent, keep your back knee on the board and only follow the upper body and arm cues.

Your arms are either up and strong or palms at the heart center.

On an exhale, lower your back knee as close to the deck pad as you can.

Keep your hips facing towards the nose of the board and rotate your upper body towards your front thigh extending your right arm forward towards the bow and your left arm back towards the tail.

Your arms and your upper body are creating a T-formation.

On an inhale, raise your back knee into your Crescent Warrior with your arms at your desired position.

Repeat the flow for about 45 seconds.

The bulk of the effort should be coming from your hips, your butt, and the sides of your body (your obliques).

Keep breathing in and out through your nose.

Adjust the speed of your movement to the level of challenge that you want but make sure you do not sacrifice your form.

Your inhale and exhale do not need to follow your movement as long as they are performed through your nose.

If you start breathing through your mouth, slow down until you resume nose breathing.

To get out of the flow, bring your hands on your board transitioning into our High or Low Lunge and then Downward Facing Dog.

Prepare for the other side.

Figure 44: Flying Crescent with Right Leg Forward

Figure 45: Flying Crescent with Right Leg Forward, different angle

Five-Pointed Star

Start in our High Lunge with your right leg back, facing the nose of your board and your upper body within the Sweet Spot.

Bring your left hand on the inside of left foot using just the fingertips for support.

Set your back foot flat on the board, with the toes pointing towards the nose/right rail at about 45-degree angle.

Straighten your back knee pushing through the outside of the foot towards the tail of the board. Pretend you are lifting the thigh muscles. This way you are using the strength of the right side of the butt, while taking pressure off your back knee.

Now, squeeze your glutes and brace the rest of your core straightening the left knee as well and raising your upper body towards the sky.

Your upper body should be within the Sweet Spot of your board. If it is not, adjust the position of your feet accordingly.

Turn both feet out to the side; you are aiming for 90-degree angle. So your left toes point to the nose and the right toes to the tail.

Activate your glutes by pushing through your heels and the outside of the feet on your board.

Extend your arms out to the sides, so that they are parallel to the board. Your left arm points towards the nose and the right arm towards the tail. Squeeze your fingertips together to engage more of your triceps.

Your shoulders should be down and back, away from the ears and your chest open.

Keep your chin and your gaze slightly up.

If it feels good on your neck, look up towards the sky, otherwise look wherever it makes your neck comfortable and helps you stay balanced.

Hold the pose for about 4 breaths focusing on nose breathing.

To get out of the pose, turn to the face the nose of the board. Bend your front knee, windmill down and pivot on your back toes, bringing your hands on your board (on either side of your left foot), transitioning into our High Lunge and Downward Facing Dog.

Figure 46 Five Pointed Star

Goddess

Come into our Five-Pointed Star facing the right rail of your board, with you torso within the Sweet Spot.

Bring your hands on your hips and bending your knees at about 90 degrees, lower into a squat, letting your butt go as far back as it needs to, for your thighs to be parallel to the board.

Keep your upper body straight. Do not hinge from your hips or your waist.

Activate your glutes by pushing through your heels and the outside of the feet on your board.

Do not allow the knees to roll in. Keep them inline with the heels. If you need to, narrow your stance by bringing your feet closer and still keeping the toes turned out.

Now inhale and extend your arms up over your head and on an exhale, bend the arms at the elbows, palms face the ears or in front of you, which ever way feels best on your shoulders, back and chest.

Keep your chest open looking into the horizon.

If you feel pressure on your lower back you can bring the hands to the heart center or rest them on your thighs.

Hold for 4 breaths focusing on nose breathing.

To get out of the pose, inhale, straighten the knees and extend the arms parallel to your board, coming into our Five Pointed Start.

Figure 47: Goddess

Warrior II – Left Leg Forward

Our Warrior II is all about the glutes and the legs.

Start in our High Lunge with your right leg back, facing the nose of your board and your upper body within the Sweet Spot.

Set your back foot flat on the board, with the toes pointing towards the nose/right rail at about 45-degree angle.

Straighten your back knee pushing through the outside of the foot towards the tail of the board. Pretend you are lifting the thigh muscles. This way you are using the strength of the right side of the butt, while taking pressure off your back knee.

Raise your upper body towards the sky, keeping your shoulders down and back, away from the ears.

Your upper body should be within the Sweet Spot of your board. If it is not, adjust the position of your feet accordingly.

Your front knee is bent so that your front thigh is as parallel to the board as possible. Keep your toes pointing straight towards the nose of the board and your front knee right above the heel. Push your front heel onto your board feeling the left side of the butt.

Extend your left arm towards the nose of the board and your right arm towards the tail, palms facing the board. Squeeze your fingertips together to engage more of your triceps. If that is too much pressure on your lower back, bring the hands to the heart center.

To get the most benefits out of this pose, keep your hips as low as possible. Keeping your hips low and your lunge deep is also assisting you to stay more balanced on your board.

Keep your chin and your gaze slightly up.

If it feels good on your neck, look towards the nose of the board, otherwise look wherever it makes your neck comfortable and helps you stay balanced.

Hold the pose for about 4 breaths focusing on nose breathing.

To get out of the pose, windmill down and pivot on your back toes, bringing your hands on your board, on either side of your front foot, transitioning into our High Lunge and Downward Facing Dog.

Prepare for the other side.

Figure 48: Warrior II with Right Leg Forward

Reclined Warrior – Left Leg Forward

Our Reclined Warrior is all about the glutes and the legs.

Start in our High Lunge pose with the left leg forward, facing the nose of the board.

Place yours hands wherever you need, using only the fingertips for support, if possible.

Set your back foot flat on the board with the toes pointing towards the nose/right rail at about 45-degree angle.

Bend your front knee (left) so that the front thigh is as parallel to the board as possible. The toes are pointing straight towards the nose of the board and your front knee is above the heel.

Raise your upper body up towards the sky, facing the right rail.

Your upper body should be within the Sweet Spot of your board. If it is not, adjust the position of your feet accordingly.

Lower your left arm on your back thigh (right) and extend your left arm up, over your head and back towards the tail of the board, working your oblique muscles.

Keep your neck relaxed looking towards wherever it helps you stay balanced.

Keep the back leg straight and the back foot still turned in at about 45 degrees.

Activate the back thigh, and keep pushing through the outside of the back foot, activating the right side of the glutes.

Keep the front leg into a deep lunge, and keep pushing the front heel and the board activating the left side of the glutes.

Keep your shoulders away from your ears.

Hold the Reclined Warrior for about 4 breaths, while breathing in and out through the nose.

To get out of the pose, windmill down, pivot on your back toes, setting your hands on your board, on either side of your front foot and go back into our High Lunge.

Repeat on the other side.

Figure 49: Reclined Warrior with Right Leg Forward

Bent Knee Triangle – Left Leg Forward

Our Bent Knee Triangle is all about the glutes and the legs.

Start in our High Lunge with your right leg back, facing the nose of your board and your upper body within the Sweet Spot.

Bring your left hand on the inside of the left foot using just the fingertips for support.

Set your back foot flat on the board, with the toes pointing towards the nose/right rail at about 45-degree angle.

Straighten your back knee pushing through the outside of the foot towards the tail of the board. Pretend you are lifting the thigh muscles. This way you are using the strength of the right side of the butt, while taking pressure off your back knee.

Keep the fingertips of your left hand on the board for support, if you need to, and extend your right arm straight up towards the sky opening up your chest towards the right rail of your board.

Your upper body should be within the Sweet Spot of your board. If it is not, adjust the position of your feet accordingly.

Your front knee is bent so that your front thigh is as parallel to the board as possible. Keep your toes pointing straight towards the nose of the board and your front knee right above the heel. Push your front heel onto your board feeling the left side of the butt.

Keep your hips as low as possible. Keeping your hips low and your lunge deep is also assisting you to stay more balanced on your board.

Now to get the most out of our Bent Knee Triangle, it is very important that you fully engage your legs, your glutes and the rest of your core so that you get your lower hand off the board and use your own strength to support you.

Do not apply pressure on your left leg with your left arm. Use your core for strength, not your legs for leverage.

Keep reaching up towards the sky and down towards the board with equal strength, opening up the chest. Your palms are facing towards the right rail of your board. Squeeze your fingertips together to engage more of your triceps.

Your shoulders should be down and back, away from the ears.

Keep your chin and your gaze slightly up.

If it feels good on your neck, look up towards the sky, otherwise look wherever it makes your neck comfortable and helps you stay balanced.

Hold the pose for about 4 breaths focusing on nose breathing.

To get out of the pose, windmill down and pivot on your back toes, bringing your hands on your board, on either side of your left foot, transitioning into our High Lunge and Downward Facing Dog.

Prepare for the other side.

Figure 50: Bent knee triangle with Right Leg Forward

Bent Knee Side Angle – Left Leg Forward

Our Bent Knee Side Angle is all about the glutes and the legs.

Start in our High Lunge with your right leg back, facing the nose of your board and your upper body within the Sweet Spot.

Bring your left hand on the inside of your left foot using just the fingertips for support.

Set your back foot flat on the board, with the toes pointing towards the nose/right rail at about 45-degree angle.

Straighten your back knee pushing through the outside of the foot towards the tail of the board. Pretend you are lifting the thigh muscles. This way you are using the strength of the right side of the butt, while taking pressure off your back knee.

Set your left forearm on your front thigh for support.

Now reach with your right arm straight up towards the sky, turn the palm to face the nose of the board and point your arm towards the nose of your board creating one powerful straight line from the outside of your right foot to the fingertips of your right hand.

Keep opening up your chest towards the right rail of your board, do not let it collapse.

Your upper body should be within the Sweet Spot of your board. If it is not, adjust the position of your feet accordingly.

Your front knee is bent so that your front thigh is as parallel to the board as possible. Keep your toes pointing straight towards the nose of the board and your front knee right above the heel. Push your front heel onto your board feeling the left side of the butt.

Keep your hips as low as possible. Keeping your hips low and your lunge deep is also assisting you to stay more balanced on your board.

Now to get the most out of our Bent Knee Side Angle, it is very important that you fully engage your legs, your glutes and the rest of your core so that you get your front forearm off your thigh and use your own strength to support you. Turn your left palm to face the sky and point your arm towards the right rail of the board.

If you are going to keep your left forearm on your thigh, do not apply any pressure on your left leg with your left arm. Use your core for strength, not your legs for leverage.

Your shoulders should be down and back, away from the ears.

Keep your chin and your gaze slightly up; if possible, towards the direction that makes your neck comfortable and helps you stay balanced.

Hold the pose for about 4 breaths focusing on nose breathing.

To get out of the pose, first set your left forearm on your thigh for support; Windmill down, pivot on your back toes, bring your hands on your board, on either side of your left foot, and transition into our High Lunge and Downward Facing Dog.

Prepare for the other side.

Figure 51: Bent Knee Side Angle with Front Leg Support; Right Leg Forward

Figure 52: Bent Knee Side Angle without Front Leg Support

Floating Seagull – Left Leg Forward

Start in our Downward Facing Dog, facing the nose of your board.

On an inhale, bring your left leg forward, bend the knee and set it on the board.

Extend your right leg back with the toes tucked under or the top of your foot on your deck pad, whichever way feels best on your foot.

Bring your left foot as far forward as you can, so that the hips come as close to the board as possible, without any pain on your joints.

It is very important that you do not apply any force on your hips and knees.

Using your hands for support on your board or your left leg, keep your upper body raised towards the sky.

To get the most out of this pose, keep your butt loose.

Your hips can shift towards the side that feels the best on your thighs, hips and glutes (as always, "best" does not imply "easiest". :-))

You can drop your head back or keep it up, which ever way feels best on your neck.

Hold for no longer than 4 breaths, focusing on nose breathing.

To get out of the pose, on an exhale, bring your left leg back transitioning into our Downward Facing Dog.

Bicycle your feet and prepare for the other side.

Figure 53: Floating Seagull, Right Leg Forward

Figure 54: Floating Seagull Variation, hands on the front leg

Camel

Come into our Tabletop facing the nose of the board.

On an inhale, get your hands off the board, standing on your knees, with your toes tucked under. This should feel really good on the bottom of your feet and your toes. If it doesn't, set the top of your feet on your board.

Bring your hands behind your lower back to support it and gently push hips and thighs forward. Feel your backbend, but do not force it. Your backbend is created by pushing hips and thighs forward.

You can drop your head back or keep it up, which ever way feels best on your neck.

If you wish to go deeper into the pose, you can reach for your heels with your hands. If your toes are tucked under, it is less of a distance than with the top of the feet on the board.

Hold for 4 breaths. If you need to breathe through the mouth during your backbend, please do that.

To get out of the pose, supporting your lower back with your hands, gently inhale into standing straight on your knees and exhale into our Cat pose.

Figure 55: Camel with hands supporting the lower back

Figure 56: Camel reaching for the heels with toes tucked under

Figure 57: Camel reaching for the heels with top of the feet on the ground

One Legged Seated Forward Fold – Left Leg Extended

Come sitting within the Sweet Spot of your board.

Use your hands to adjust your butt so that your pelvis is tilting forward. It will help you to get the most out of our Seated Forward Fold.

Bend your right knee, keep it on the board, and set the bottom of your right foot on the inside of your left thigh, as close to the groin area as possible.

Keep your left foot flexed (toes pointing to the sky).

On an inhale, raise your arms up towards the sky and on an exhale, hinging from your hips gently lower your upper body towards your lower body.

If you can reach your left foot, interlace your fingers and grab around the bottom of your foot with your hands. Otherwise, rest your hands on your board wherever they can reach at.

If you can, bring your chin towards the chest and feel your body extending all the way from the back of your left leg through your whole spine to the back of your neck.

Hold the pose for no longer than 4 breaths focusing on nose breathing.

To get out of the pose, use your right arm and gently extend your right leg forward.

Shake both legs a couple of times, rearrange your pelvis (tilting forward) and prepare for the other side.

Figure 58: One Legged Seated Forward Fold, Right Leg Forward

Easy Sitting Pose

Come sitting on your board, within your Sweet Spot, facing the nose.

Extend your legs forward, shake them a couple of times, bend your knees and cross your legs.

You can cross the legs in two different ways: One leg can be underneath the other or in front of the other.

Your knees should be as far out to the side as you can, to open up your hips.

Adjust your butt so that your pelvis is tilting forward. This will help your spine stay tall.

Keep your shoulders down, away from your ears.

Place your hands on your thighs, palms facing up or down, depending on what feels best for your shoulders.

Gaze into the horizon and focus on your nose breathing.

Hold for about 4 breaths.

To get out of the pose, use your arms to support your legs, extend your legs forward, shake them a couple of times and repeat with the legs crossed the other way (which ever leg was on top or in front goes underneath or behind.)

By bringing your hands in front of you, onto the board, you can very smoothly transition into our Table Top.

Figure 59: Easy Sitting

Rock Pose

Come into our Table Top with your upper body within the Sweet Spot of your board.

Bring your butt towards your heels and see if your butt can touch your heels.

If this seems too difficult (due to discomfort on your knees, lower back, the top of your feet on the deck pad, etc.), please, do not force it. Substitute with our Easy Sitting instead.

If it feels easy, proceed with it and come sitting on your heels.

Keep your spine straight, your shoulders down, place the back of one hand inside the palm of the other and let your hands rest on your lap.

If you would like to go deeper into this pose, tuck your toes under, so that your heels are now higher and you are working on extending the bottom of your feet. Keep in mind that this may feel really uncomfortable. :-)

Hold for about 4 breaths.

To get out of the pose, on an exhale, lower your butt on your deck pad, to the left side of your feet, extend your legs forward, shake them a couple of times and come into our Easy Sitting.

Figure 60: Rock Pose with top of the feet on the ground

Figure 61: Rock Pose with toes tucked under

Neck Stretches

Come sitting comfortably in our Rock Pose or Easy Sitting Cross Legged. It is best if you can sit into our Rock Pose.

Keep your spine tall and your shoulders down away from your ears.

Our neck stretches is a set of movements that work the neck in 4 different ways:

Movement 1

- Bring your chin to your chest rounding the back of your neck.
- Look up towards the sky arching the back of your neck;
- Repeat 4 times.

Figure 62: Chin to the chest

Figure 63: Look up towards the sky

Movement 2
- Look left, with your neck.
- Look right, with your neck.
- Repeat 4 times.

Figure 64: Look left with your neck

Figure 65: Look right with your neck

Movement 3
- Bring your left ear towards your left shoulder.
- Come back to center.
- Bring your right ear towards your right shoulder.
- Come back to center.
- Repeat 4 times.

Figure 66: Left ear towards the left shoulder

Figure 67: Right ear towards the right shoulder

Movement 4

- Bring your chin to your chest.

- Very slowly create 2 large circles in one direction; gently moving through any tension you may have on the back of your neck. Make the circles as large and as complete as you can, without applying any force.

- When your chin reaches the bottom of the 2 circles, repeat in the opposite direction.

- When you have completed both sets, bring your chin to your chest, interlace your fingers behind your neck and using only the weight of your arms, bring your chin towards your chest rounding your neck and your spine as you close your elbows together.

- On an inhale open up your chest as much as you can, separating the elbows.

- Keep your fingers interlaced, turn the palms to face the sky, and extend your arms over your head, looking up towards the sky.

- On an exhale, bring your hands to your heart center and release by your sides.

Figure 68: On an inhale pen up the chest as much as you can

Seated Spinal Twist – Left Leg Extended

Come sitting within the Sweet Spot of your board.

Keep your left leg extended forward and wrap your right leg over your left, setting your right foot flat on the board on the outside of your left knee.

Bring your right hand on your board, behind you, close to your butt in order to keep your spine straight.

On an inhale, extend your left arm over your head and on an exhale wrap it outside your right thigh with the palm facing away from you.

Turn your upper body and your gaze towards tail of your board.

With every inhale lift your spine, with every exhale twist a little bit deeper.

Repeat for 4 breaths, focusing on nose breathing.

To get out of the pose, unwind your upper body towards the left rail. Come back to center. Extend both legs forward, shake them a couple of times and get ready for the other side.

Figure 69: Seated Spinal Twist, Right Leg Extended

Figure 70: Seated Spinal Twist, different angle

Corpse Pose

Lie on your board with your head towards the nose of your board, possibly on your life jacket. :-) This way, your hair is less likely to get wet.

Separate your legs to the distance that feels the best on your lower back.

Place your arms a few inches away from the rest of your body, palms facing the sky or the board, depending on what feels best on your shoulders.

Lift your head a couple of inches off the board and set it back down, helping your cervical spine extend sinking into the board (your neck area.)

Lift your butt a couple of inches off the board and set it back down, helping your lumbar spine extend sinking into the board (your lower back area.)

Now focus at your nose breathing holding the pose for about 4 breaths.

To get out of our Corpse pose, bend your knees and hug them as close to your chest as you can and very gently, without falling into the water, unless you wish to, rock from side to side, massaging your lower back.

Roll over into your favorite side, and using both arms for support, come into our Easy Sitting.

Figure 71: Corpse Pose

The Sexy Seven

"Attachment is that which dwells on pleasure. We are never attached to that in which we do not find pleasure. We find pleasure in very queer things, sometimes, but the principle remains that whatever object, we find pleasure in, to that we are attached. - Raja Yoga by Swami Vivekananda, Ramakrishna-Vivekananda Center New York (p.147)

Staying On Your Path

The Sexy Seven are 7 categories of poses that may sound and / or look "pretty" on the board but have hidden risks. Their Ratio is typically higher than 2, which means that their risk is twice as high as the reward. Risk means anywhere from serious injury to fatality. We also refer to them as "high-maintenance" poses.

We suggest that you do no teach these poses to clients on a paddleboard. Also, if you are not 100% comfortable performing these poses on land and in a controlled environment, we highly recommend that you do not attempt them on the water.

The 7 Categories Of The High-Maintenance Poses

1. Restorative Yoga

Restorative Yoga is based on the principles of relaxation, as in no movement, no effort, the brain is quiet. To relax is to rest deeply.

In "The Wellness Book", Herbert Benson, M.D., who coined the phrase "Relaxation Response", defines it as "a physiological state characterized by a slower heart rate, metabolism, rate of breathing, lower blood pressure, and slower brain wave patterns."

Restorative yoga aims to achieve this by putting the body in a comfortable position, through the use of props (blocks, bolsters, blankets, etc.). Poses are held for at least a few minutes at a time or longer, allowing you to open your body through passive stretching. From everything we discussed in the previous chapters you can see why a Restorative Yoga practice on the paddleboard is classified as counter-productive or potentially injurious.

2. Yin Yoga

Yin Yoga is based on the principles of fascia (connective tissue) and self-myofascial release. The goal of Yin Yoga is to structurally and energetically open and re-hydrate the human fascial system. The human fascial system is the carrier of frequency, vibration, information and organization necessary for the health and quality of life. Its condition is immediately reflected in anywhere from the strength and mobility of our joints and ligaments to the state of our mind and emotions.

There are two elements essential to Yin Yoga: Time and Pressure. Gentle pressure, applied over time, allows the fascia to rehydrate and elongate.

During a Yin Yoga practice the poses (specific type of "floor-based" poses) are held for a few minutes, on average, anywhere between 2 minutes to 5 minutes, depending on the individual. These specific Yin poses cause isometric pressure to be applied to the target area, typically the hips, lower back and shoulders. For the pressure to be effective, all of the muscles and tendons at and surrounding the target area need to be fully relaxed. Any contraction is going to undermine and even reverse the effects of the pose, causing injury, whether short term or long term.

As we already mentioned earlier, any physical movement on an unstable surface, inherently causes all of our muscles to contract, which in turn helps us develop strength. Any Yin-type poses involving long holds are counter to the inherent nature of the paddleboard.

A Yin Yoga practice, performed on the paddleboard would be classified as counter-productive or potentially injurious. All Yin style poses, on the paddleboard, should not be held for longer than a few seconds and should only be performed as a break in between strength and balance targeting poses.

3. Flexibility oriented poses simultaneously involving multiple joints

Poses that require multiple of our joints to simultaneously go in a position that is against what our body spends the day in, while on an unstable surface and in an uncontrolled environment can cause serious injury. Examples of such poses are: Wheel, Reclined Hero aka Fixed Firm, Warrior I, etc.

4. Poses that compress vulnerable joint areas

Our neck and lower back are very vulnerable areas. Poses that compress these joints, while on an unstable surface and in an uncontrolled environment can cause serious injuries. Examples of such poses are: Fish, Shoulder Stand, Plow, Head Stand, etc.

5. Poses that require locking the joints in load bearing situations

Poses that require us to lock our joints while bearing load on an unstable surface and in an uncontrolled environment can cause serious injuries. Examples of such poses are: Triangle, Standing Head to Knee, etc.

6. Revolved poses that involve compressing and locking joints simultaneously

Revolved poses that require us to simultaneously compress and lock the joints while on an unstable surface and in an uncontrolled environment can cause serious injuries. Example of such poses is: Revolved Triangle.

7. Binding poses

Binding poses that may overly stretch joint areas, especially for people with shorter limbs or not the "right" proportions for the pose, while on an unstable surface and in an uncontrolled environment can cause serious injuries. Example of such poses is: Bound Triangle.

The Destination Poses

"An increase of speed, an increase of struggle, is able to bridge the gulf of time. That which naturally takes a long time to accomplish can be shortened by the intensity of the action..." - *Raja Yoga by Swami Vivekananda, Ramakrishna-Vivekananda Center New York (p. 45)*

Get Out Of Your Comfort Zone - Flow Into Your Destination Pose

The Destination Poses, is what drives us, keeps us motivated, and adds spice to our yoga practice and beyond! A Destination Pose is very personal, contemporary and relative. A Destination Pose for one person may not necessarily be a Destination Pose for some one else. It all depends on "how hard" it is for the practitioner, at the time, in terms of their strength and balance.

The question now becomes, "how hard should it be?" Answers vary, but the general thinking is about 4 percent. That's it. If you want to get the most out of your SUP & Yoga practice, to get into that meditative state, the challenge should be 4 percent greater than your skills.

The keywords here are "challenge" and "skill". You achieve way more, a lot faster and a lot safer, physically, mentally and emotionally by mastering your "skills" at each level (within your comfort zone) before moving on to the "challenge" of the next level (beyond your comfort zone.)

Mastering your skills at each level simply means mastering your strength and balance abilities of your SUP & Yoga practice.

Challenging yourselves beyond your comfort zone, means choose a pose that requires more strength and balance than what you are already familiar and comfortable with and master that one.

When we don't know what is coming next, we pay more attention, we concentrate. Paying attention, concentrating is our vehicle, our ride to meditation.

Examples of Destination Poses

There are many Destination Poses out there. Here is a list of just a few:

- Arm Balancing Poses (such as crow and handstand)
- One-legged Balancing Poses (such as Dancer, Warrior III and One-legged Chair)
- Wild Thing

Since as we already said, most of the Destination Poses are very personal, we are only going to give cues for Wild Thing.

Wild Thing Pose - One Side

Start in our Reverse Table Top pose, with your upper body within the Sweet Spot.

Extend your right leg as straight as you can, turning your right toes out to the side, pointing towards the right rail of your board.

Push your right hand onto the board, turning the fingers to point towards the tail/right rail of your board.

Bend your left knee a little bit more and bring your left foot further back on your board, underneath your left hip, turning the toes out to the side.

Let your left hand come off the board, but keep extending it towards the tail of your board.

Keep squeezing your glutes and engaging the rest of your core, lifting the hips and the chest as high off the board as you can.

Keep your neck loose.

Hold the pose for no more than 4 breaths, as long as there is no pressure on your lower back.

To get out of the pose, transition into our Reverse Table Top.

Repeat on the opposite side.

Figure 72: Wild Thing, Left Leg Extended

Breath Work On the Board

"To get that subtle perception we have to begin with the grosser perceptions. We have to get hold of that which is setting the whole engine in motion; that is prana, the most obvious manifestation of which is the breath. Then, along with the breath, we shall slowly enter into the body, and thus be able to find out about the subtle forces, ..."
- *Raja Yoga by Swami Vivekananda, Ramakrishna-Vivekananda Center New York (p. 30)*

It is not hard to guess that your paddleboard on the water is one of the most ideal settings on earth for breath work. Even more so, if the waterway happens to be on a moving body of water. And even though as of the writing of this book, according to Wikipedia "Breathwork has no verified beneficial effect on health", there is a lot of evidence out there that demonstrates otherwise.

We invite you to do your own research, conduct your own experiments and come to your own conclusions.

Nevertheless, after implementing all of the following practices, you will have discovered for yourself how much fun, breath work on the paddleboard really is!

Yin Breathing Pattern

To get the most out of your paddling, it is important to first make a habit of the following simple practices:

- ◆ Keeping your shoulders down and your arms straight to assist your chest and diaphragm to expand. This way your breaths become deeper and fuller.

- ◆ Focusing on both your inhale and exhale being through the nose. The easiest way to achieve this is to make a conscious effort of keeping your mouth closed. Having said that, please, do not suffocate. If you need to take a breath through your mouth, please, do so.

There is a significant amount of research which shows that full breaths, in and out through the nose, assist your nervous system to stay calm leading to more sustained energy.

Our Yin Breathing Pattern described above is based on our Yin Paddling Technique. For a detailed explanation of our Yin Paddling technique, please refer to our **"Walk On Water - A Guide To Flat Water Stand Up Paddling" book.**

Breathing Exercises

If you thought that practicing yoga poses on the board was really fun, wait until you perform breathing exercises on the board.

In the following sections we explore the most effective and efficient breathing exercises that are also very conducive to the paddleboard.

Belly Breathing

You can practice our Belly Breathing while in any pose. However, the 3 poses that we have found work best to begin with, are: Our Easy Sitting, Rock Pose and Corpse Pose.

Choose any of the 3 poses mentioned above. Place one hand on your belly and your other hand on your chest.
Exhale through your nose; letting as much air out of your lungs as you can and notice how your belly goes in, in other words it shrinks like a balloon. Focal point of contraction is the solar plexus, the junction between the rib case and the abdominal muscles. Abdominal contraction pushes the abdomen up against the diaphragm and lower lobes of the lungs, squeezing CO_2 out.

Now inhale through your nose, allowing as much air into your lungs as you can and notice how your belly goes out, in other words, it expands like a balloon.

Try to keep your chest from moving. The less your chest moves and the more your belly expands and shrinks (I.e. the more you engage the abdominal muscles), the fuller your breathing becomes.

Complete 4 full breaths like this and return into your regular nose breathing.

Alternate Nostril Breathing

As the name implies, you are going to breathe through one nostril at a time, in an alternating manner. A full breath is an exhale followed by an inhale. You can use either hand to assist you in closing the nostrils. For the sake of explanation we will use the right hand, in particular the thumb to close the right nostril and the index finger to close the left nostril. You can also use the thumb to close the right nostril and the ring and pinky fingers together to close the left nostril.

Sit comfortably on your board, in easy sitting, or rock pose. Keep your spine tall and your shoulders down and away from the ears.

Relax your belly.

Take 3-4 deep belly breaths.

After a full inhale:

- Using your right thumb to close the right nostril, and exhale through the left.
- Keeping the right nostril blocked with the thumb, inhale through the left nostril.
- Block your left nostril, with the index finger (or ring and pinky) open your right nostril and exhale through the right.
- Keeping your left nostril blocked, inhale through the right.
- Block your right nostril, with the thumb, open your left nostril and exhale through the left.

Repeat for at least two minutes or longer.

Studies have showed that consistent practice over about a month tends to lower heart rate and blood pressure. Studies have also showed that it has balancing effect on the functional activity of the brain's hemispheres.

Breath Of Power (Kapalabhati)

Often categorized as a purification exercise, not breathing exercise.

It basically feels like you are "blowing your nose".

You force the exhale and the inhale happens as a reflex, you do not need to actively inhale. The short exhale is primarily generated by a sharp contraction of the lower belly muscle. The relatively longer inhale results from a relaxation of this contraction.

The Breath of Power cleanses the sinuses, respiratory passages and lungs and keeps the spongy tissue of the lungs supple. It strengthens, massages and tones the abdominal muscles and organs including the diaphragm and liver. It improves the digestion.

In general, it is a good practice to do 2 rounds of Kapalabhati of about 20-30 repetitions each.

Always follow Kapalabhati breathing by Alternate Nostril Breathing. Kapalabhati breathing helps cleanse the body from free radicals and alternate nostril breathing helps you ground.

Ocean Breath (Ujjayi Prāṇāyāma)

A little bit of anatomy before we move forward with the Ocean Breath. You may or may not have heard of a very interesting part of our body called the glottis. The glottis is the narrowed aperture in the pharynx located at the level of the vocal chords that automatically closes when we swallow food or saliva. Normally, we open and close the glottis unconsciously. Consciously narrowing the opening of the glottis increases the turbulence of the air passing through the cavities. This raises the temperature of the air above normal. It also creates an audible vibration. We voluntarily constrict the glottis any time we stand in front of a mirror and try to fog it by a strong exhale.

The Ocean Breath is basically the breathing technique where the inhale and the exhale still happen through the nose while the glottis is being constricted to make an ocean-like sound.

This is the type of breathing that you may eventually incorporate during your whole yoga practice on the board. It will help keep you warm in colder conditions and break a sweat in warmer conditions.

Breath Work Tip

Remember that breathing directly reflects our mental and emotional state. When our breathing is restless or uneven, it reflects our distracted mind. When our breathing is subtle and slow, it reflects our concentrated sate of mind. In reality, our mind is most focused when we are neither inhaling nor exhaling. During the pause between an unforced exhalation and the next inhalation, we are the most calm and our mind most able to focus on subtle things. We all experience this "breathless state" but we are usually unaware of it.

The "normal" rate of breathing is about 16 times a minute. An experienced meditator breathes 2-3 times in a minute, or even less.

Meditation

"When all the motions of the body have become perfectly rhythmical, the body becomes a gigantic battery of will." - Raja Yoga by Swami Vivekananda, Ramakrishna-Vivekananda Center New York (p. 54)

Being on the water in any way is cleansing in and of itself. If you now combine the water, the rhythm of nature, the effects of meditative practices and the instability of the board, you receive a complete body, mind and spirit rejuvenating experience.

Breath and attention are two of your best tools to reach that meditative state (the zone). In the previous chapter you became familiar with the Yin Breathing Technique. The next step is to start paying attention to your paddling. This is really easy to do, let's see how.

Moving Meditation

Think of it as the difference between mechanics versus awareness. While paddling, ask yourselves the following questions:

- Are you present on your board or is your mind somewhere else?

- Can you feel the resistance of the water against your board and your paddle?

- Are you aware of the speed you are moving at, if at all?

- Are you aware of the direction your are moving towards, if at all?

- Are you using your body mechanically or are you really being aware of your movement?

- If some one asked you what part of your body is doing the most work would you be able to answer definitively or would you be guessing and having to think about it?

- Can you feel the air against your skin and which direction the wind is blowing, if at all?

- Are you aware of your surrounding scenery, smells and sounds?

If your mind is quiet enough, focused enough and present enough, all of the above questions will be easy to answer. If your mind is not quiet, focused or present enough, by asking yourself the above questions, you have just brought yourself into a "moving meditation" state.

Mantra Meditation

The concept of mantra is so widely spread that the term mantra has pretty much entered the English vocabulary. According to the Merriam-Webster online dictionary mantra is "a sound, word, or phrase that is repeated by someone who is praying or meditating: a word or phrase that is repeated often or that expresses someone's basic beliefs."

What the above definition basically says is that words, when used with intention, carry power. Let's take a moment to explore the etymology of mantra in order to better understand its uses.

In Sanskrit, the language that the word originated in, "man" means "to think" and "tra" designates tools or instruments. Hence, mantra is an instrument of thought. Also, in Sanskrit again, "manas" is the mind and "tra" means to protect. Therefore, mantra could be translated as, that which protects the mind.

We could think of mantra as a word or phrase that we repeat to ourselves again and again, eliminating all the other random thoughts, in order to be able to focus on a specific effect.

It is that repetition which creates the rhythm in our mind eventually leading to concentration and even meditation.

By now you should be wondering whether you have to learn Sanskrit to make use of mantras.

The answer is no, you do not have to learn any new language, even though learning a new language might sound to some of you as an exciting thought!

Any word or phrase that cultivates a positive quality, thought or feeling may be used for mantra meditation. We may use a mantra for health, for love, for compassion, for will power, to overcome obstacles, to conquer any fears or simply to rest our mind. Your mantra can stay the same for a while or change daily according to your needs. You can choose to repeat your mantra either verbally or mentally, whichever way works best for you.

As you can tell, paddleboarding, practicing SUP & Yoga or simply hanging out on your board is a perfect setting for mantra meditation. So, get on your board, choose your mantra and enjoy the ride! It is your mantra, your thought, your need, yours for whatever you want it to be.

Mudrā Meditation

The term mudrā may not be as familiar to you as that of mantra. Its concept however is innate to your human nature. The Sanskrit word mudrā translates to hand gesture or hand seal to be exact. Think about it… Any time you use your hands to express yourselves, make a point during a conversation, help you recall something, or simply focus, you are using a mudrā.

What you are subconsciously doing with those hand gestures is seal energy in your body to prevent it from leaking out and from being wasted. By subconsciously sealing our hands together, we symbolically close and therefore activate an energetic self-circuit.

As you are probably guessing, this exact same practice can also be applied consciously and intentionally with even stronger results. We all know that any time we use attention and intention the effects are manifold.

Below we are going to explore 3 different mudrās that lend themselves very graciously to your time on the paddleboard.

Heart Seal - Añjali Mudrā

You can practice the Heart Seal whether seated or standing.

- Bring your hands in front of your chest, press your open palms and fingers together and rest the sides of your joined thumbs against your sternum, in a prayer like gesture.

- Both hands should feel equal pressure.

- Keep your forearms parallel to the board, as you widen your elbows outwardly.

- To go even deeper into your mudrā, use the pressure of the palms to create similar action on the scapulae (your shoulder blades.) It is as if your are pressing the heads of your upper arms into your shoulder joints.

- Avoid squeezing your shoulder blades together; pretend you are spreading them apart.

Notice how the spreading of the palms helps increase the fullness of your breath. You will also be happy to know that the equal pressure of the two palms helps balance the two sides of the brain, making you feel even more grounded than typical.

Figure 73: The Heart Seal

Wisdom Seal - Jnāna Mudrā

It is best to practice the Wisdom Seal seated, whether in our easy sitting or rock pose.

- Join the tip of your thumb and index fingers on each hand, extending the rest of the fingers straight out of the palms.

- You can practice this mudrā with palms facing down softening the shoulders and calming the brain or palms facing up opening the chest and stimulating the brain.

◆

It is said that the thumb represents our Universal Self and the index finger our embodied self. The rest of the fingers represent the three main qualities of the manifested world: Existence (middle finger), Activity (ring finger) and Stillness (pinky finger).

This hand seal reminds us that when in this human existence, we keep the balance between activity and stillness (between doing and non-doing) it will be easier for us to experience the connection between our individual self and our collective Self.

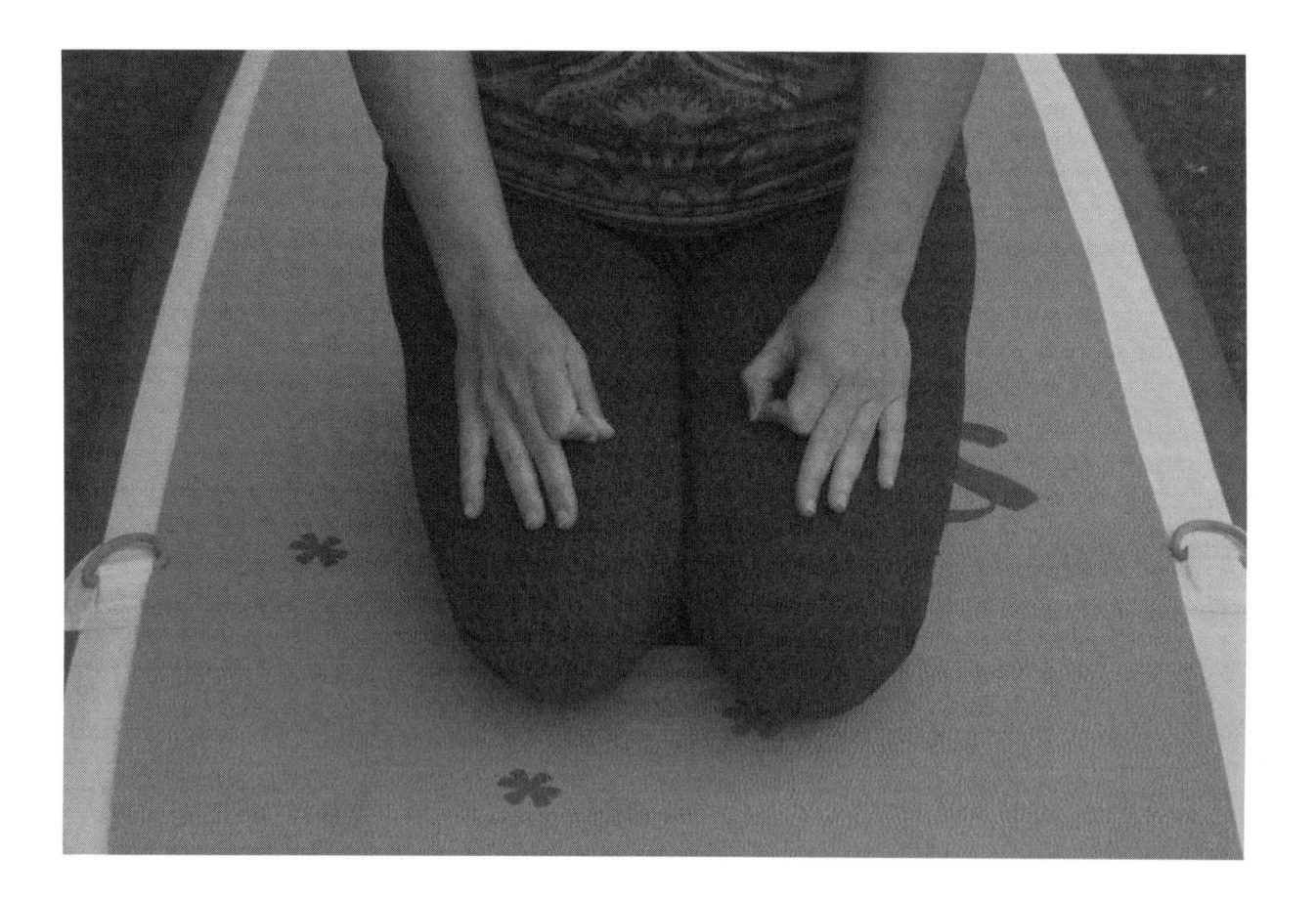

Figure 74: The Wisdom Seal, palms facing down

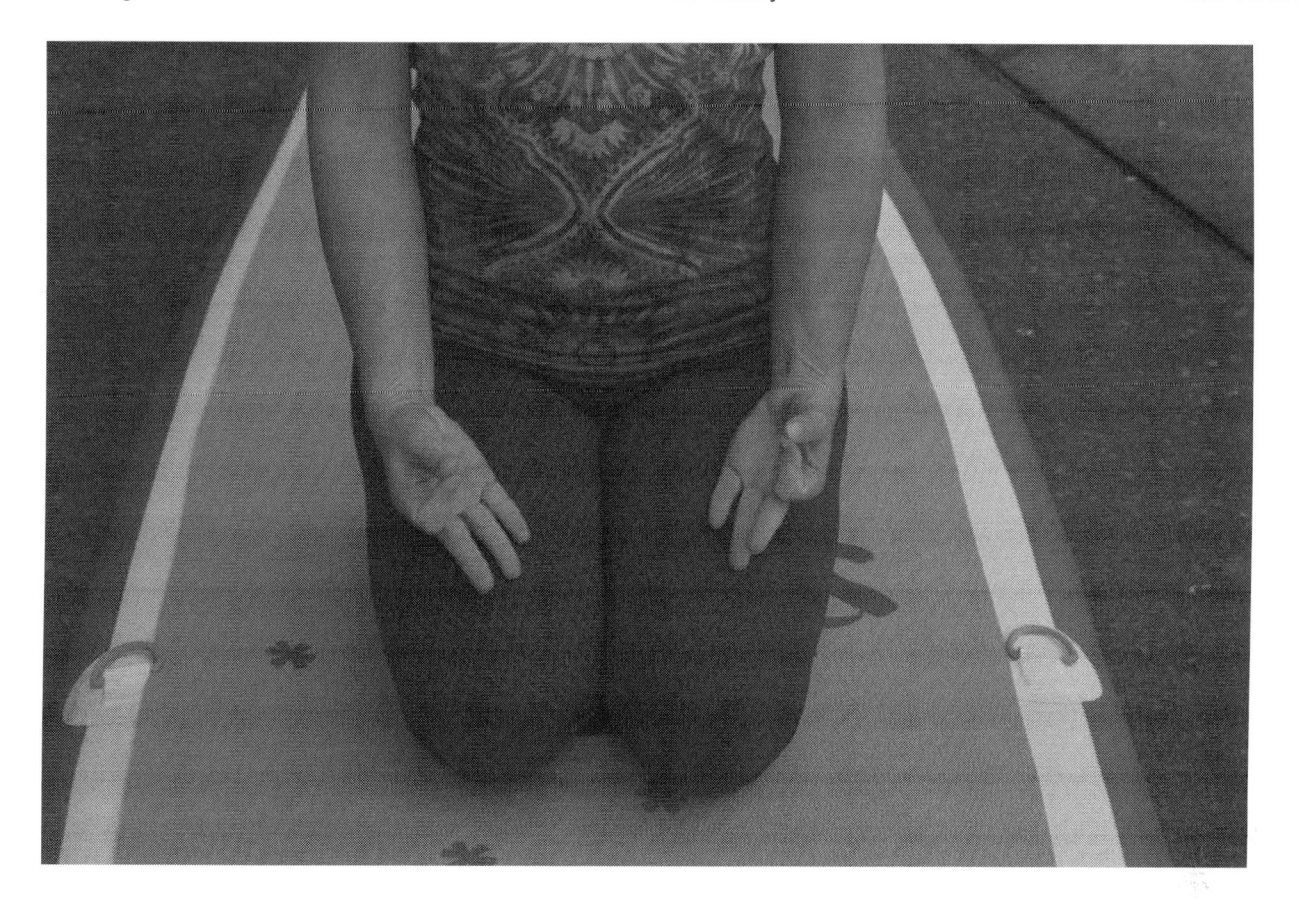

Figure 75: The Wisdom Seal, palms facing up

Meditation Seal - Dhyāna Mudrā

It is best to practice the Meditation Seal seated, whether in our easy sitting or rock pose.

- Place your hands on your lap with the back of your right hand resting in the palm of your left.

- In some traditions, the feminine version wants the back of the left hand resting in the palm of the right.

- The tips of the thumbs are lightly touching.

- You could also stack the thumbs one on top of the other.

- Keep your spine tall and your chest open.

The contact of the hands in the Meditation Seal reminds us that our focus and our inspiration become the highest when both the left and right side of our brain are working in harmony.

Figure 76: The Meditation Seal

Mudrā Meditation Tips

◆ While on your board, holding your mudrā…

◆ Relax your eyes, soften your gaze, look into the horizon or somewhere that it helps you stay focused but without intensity.

◆ Try to relax the tongue in your mouth, i.e., release the tongue from the roof of your mouth.

◆ Find your belly breathing.

- ◆ Relax your mind from random thoughts; you may incorporate the use of a mantra if you wish.

- ◆ Hand Seals remind us that every movement of the body is a ritual gesture. Enjoy your time on your board; it is your sacred ground!

The SUP & Yoga Board And Other Gear

There is no question that you can practice yoga on any board. As a matter of fact, we have practiced on anywhere from an old hybrid stand up paddleboard / kayak to a 9'8" stand up paddle surfboard.

However, if you want to make the most out of your SUP & Yoga practice, this is what you are looking for on a board.

SUP & Yoga Board Specifications

- Length that is anywhere between 10' to 11'.

- Width that is anywhere between 31" - 34".

- The thickness, i.e., the size and the shape of the rails will depend on the construction. The parameters will be different for ISUP, Plastic, EPS foam, etc.

- Light weight. This is very important. There is no use in buying a beautiful board that you cannot transport.

- Large enough "flat" area to practice on, i.e., large enough Sweet Spot.

- Full-length deck pad that is smooth, non-slippery and gentle to the skin.

- Good primary stability, i.e., the board does not tip over easily.

- Solid construction, i.e., your knee won't go through the board if you happen to fall on the board.

- A handle that does not get in the way of your practice.

- Tail that is square or slightly rounded.

- Attachments for your life jacket/whistle and paddle. It makes your practice a lot more enjoyable if you do not have to worry about what to do with your life jacket/whistle and paddle while not using them.

- Single fin with the option of it being a low profile fin when on shallow waters.

- Attachment for anchoring. It is always a good option to have. Depending on the waterways, anchoring may be desired or even needed. If you are going to anchor, choose an anchor that will not destroy your board.

Recommended Gear

When it comes to SUP & Yoga gear, please, keep in mind that when on the water, you are a Stand Up Paddler /Guide first, a Yoga Practitioner second.

This mans that it is always good practice to have Guide gear with you, not only for your own safety but for the safety of your fellow paddlers as well.

Please, refer to our **"Walk On Water - A Guide To Flat Water Stand Up Paddling"** for the detailed breakdown of the following Guide gear list.

- Leash
- Life Jacket/Whistle
- Towing System
- Carabiner
- Dry Bag
- Rock Climbing Sling
- Knife or Leatherman Wave
- Waterproof Watch
- Puka Patch – Or a high end sticker
- Cargo Area
- Proper Shoes
- Proper Clothing

The Possibilities Are Endless!

"Freedom is never to be reached by the weak; throw away all weakness. Tell your body that it is strong, tell your mind that it is strong, and have unbounded faith and hope in yourself." - Raja Yoga by Swami Vivekananda. Ramakrishna-Vivekananda Center New York (p. 33)

Now that you have been exposed to the magical world of SUP & Yoga, there is, without any doubt, no looking back. There is nothing that could stop you from making it part of your daily life. Below we are answering some of the most common questions that practitioners have asked us through the years:

Q. SUP & Yoga in a pool?

A. The right size pool with proper tie-downs is also a good possibility. Make sure that falling off the board won't cause any injuries, i.e., you won't hit the bottom or the walls of the pool. If there is more than one practitioner in the pool, the boards should have enough distance between them. If you are the teacher, you can always teach standing off the pool.

Q. SUP & Yoga indoors?

A. Yes, there is indoor SUP & Yoga, which does not require a pool. What you need is an inflatable paddleboard on top of either 2-3 Indo Cushions or 2 BOSU balls and a Kahuna Stick. The Kahuna Stick would be to simulate the paddle rotation.

Q. What about wetsuit when it is cold?

A. A wetsuit may get too warm. In that case, you might want to jump in the water and get wet more often. Do your clothing research; there are great new materials out there now. Hydroskin is one of our favorites.

Q. Too windy for SUP & Yoga?

A. Weather conditions with wind above 12 mph are not conducive to SUP & Yoga. In that case, we recommend that you implement either of the two following strategies:

- ◆ Become familiar with as many different locations in your area as possible. While the wind, waves, current, etc., may not be ideal in one place, a few miles down the road may be a whole different story.

- ◆ Do a SUP & Yoga downwinder paddle, in other words, safely, go with the wind. Just make sure you coordinate the cars/rides properly between your put-in and take-out areas.

Q. What about safety? What could go wrong?

A. Please, refer to the Safety Tips and Guiding Principles in our **"Walk On Water - A Guide To Flat Water Stand Up Paddling"** book. There is a reason we wrote that first!

Q. Anything else I need to know?

A. SUP & Yoga is NOT just yoga on the paddleboard. It is stand up paddling, it is practicing poses, it is meditating, it is breathing, it is enjoying nature, it is getting out of your comfort zone, it is communion with your inner self, it is a way of life.

Epilogue

A Note from Tim

Water has always been an integral part of my life whether canoeing and skim boarding (at age 7), sea kayaking, white water kayaking, sailing (racing Hobie Cats), scuba diving, stand up paddleboarding, surfing, serving in the Coast Guard (five years) rescue diving and boat operating for law enforcement agencies. It all started growing up on Lake Huron, where I was paddleboarding my first board, a used 7ft 2" Con Butterfly.

Through all my time on or in the water I realized that no matter who you are, water is calling you and sooner or later you are going to answer the call. Stand up paddleboarding & Yoga is one of the fun and exciting ways to do this!

Happy (Water) Trails To You!

A Note from Vie

I consider myself extremely fortunate to have been born and raised in an environment that values tradition, strength, beauty and the gift of water.

It has been my life-long passion to not only respect and embody these core values but also figure out ways to share them with as many people throughout the world as possible. Stand up paddleboarding & Yoga is one of the most effective ways I have found that can make this happen.

I welcome you and encourage you to no matter where you are, find a way, to spread the love and change lives, one paddle stroke at a time...

Stay safe!

About the Authors

Vie Binga is a lifestyle entrepreneur, outdoor adventurer and author. She loves to biohack blending science and nature, to enhance physical and mental performance, sharing her findings with others. She believes that high intention, sincere effort, and intelligent execution will always make an impact in people's lives and the world. When she is not teaching or writing, she can be found rock climbing, surfing, whitewater kayaking or scuba diving.

Tim Ganley is a lifestyle entrepreneur, outdoor adventurer and author. He loves experimenting with disciplines that lead to physical and mental strength and endurance. He believes that if people learn about the state of flow and practice building their life around it, the world will be much happier. When he is not teaching or designing new programs, he can be found white water kayaking, rock climbing, scuba diving, off road biking or surfing.

Valuable Resources

Blog posts: http://AskTimAndVie.com

How-To Videos Teacher Training Videos: YouTube.com/c/AskTimAndVie

www.LakeFun.com

We would love to hear from you!

Email: training@asktimandvie.com

Instagram: @ask_tim_and_vie

Periscope: @ask_tim_and_vie

Twitter: @ask_tim_and_vie

Facebook: AskTimAndVie

Website: AskTimAndVie.com

Bibliography

1) Walk On Water - A Guide To Flat Water Stand Up Paddling

2) **The Wellness Book: The Comprehensive Guide to Maintaining Health and Treating Stress-Related Illness, Herbert Benson, MD.**

3) **Relax and Renew By Judith Lasater, Ph.D., P.T.**

4) **The Hidden Messages in Water by Dr. Masaru Emoto**

5) **Anatomy of Hatha Yoga by H. David Coulter (2001)**

6) **Body-Mind-Spirit Integrative Medicine in Ayurveda Yoga & Nature Care by Prof. R. H. Singh (2009)**

7) **https://en.wikipedia.org/wiki/Breathwork**

8) **http://www.athleticinsight.com/Vol1Iss3/ZonePDF.pdf**

Printed in Great Britain
by Amazon